MARYLAND

Past and Present

Joanne Mattern

rosen publishing's
rosen central®

New York

Published in 2010 by The Rosen Publishing Group, Inc.
29 East 21st Street, New York, NY 10010

Library of Congress Cataloging-in-Publication Data

Mattern, Joanne, 1963–
Maryland: past and present / Joanne Mattern.—1st ed.
    p. cm.—(The United States: past and present)
Includes bibliographical references and index.
ISBN 978-1-4358-3519-1 (library binding)
ISBN 978-1-4358-8488-5 (pbk)
ISBN 978-1-4358-8489-2 (6 pack)
1. Maryland—Juvenile literature. I. Title.
F181.3.M38 2010
975.2—dc22

                                                                    2009025517

Manufactured in the United States of America

CPSIA Compliance Information: Batch #LW10YA: For Further Information contact Rosen Publishing, New York, New York at 1-800-237-9932

On the cover: Top left: Customers buy fruit and flowers at the Lexington Market, a popular shopping area in Baltimore during the late 1800s. Top right: The Maryland blue crab is the state's official crustacean and one of Maryland's tastiest products. Bottom: Baltimore's skyline rises above the waterfront, showing a modern, vibrant city.

Contents

Maryland is on the East Coast of the United States and is bordered by Pennsylvania, Delaware, West Virginia, and Virginia. Chesapeake Bay is its most distinctive physical feature.

Introduction

Maryland is a small state, but great things come in small packages. It was one of the original thirteen colonies and became the seventh state when the United States was formed. Because its history stretches back so far, Maryland has always had an important place in the nation's history.

Maryland possesses abundant geographic and natural resources. Its location along the Atlantic coast has made it a natural transportation hub. In addition, Maryland is split by a body of water called the Chesapeake Bay. The bay has brought riches and opportunities to residents as an important fishing area, a major tourist attraction, and a place of stunning natural beauty.

Maryland's location has proved valuable to the U.S. government. In 1791, Maryland gave a large tract of land for the construction of the nation's capital in a central location, one that was not under the control of any state. In 1800, that land, along with land from neighboring Virginia, became the District of Columbia. To this day, Maryland residents commute to jobs in Washington, D.C., and the state remains an important government and business center.

From its early days as a land filled with Native American settlements to its role today as a high-tech center, Maryland has changed greatly over the years. In this book, you'll discover what makes Maryland a special part of the United States.

Chapter 1

THE LAND OF MARYLAND

Maryland is one of the smallest states in the United States; it ranks forty-second in size. The total area—which includes the state's portion of the Chesapeake Bay—is 12,193 square miles (31,580 square kilometers). The state borders Pennsylvania to the north, Virginia to the south, and West Virginia to the south and west. The state of Delaware and the Atlantic Ocean provide Maryland's eastern border.

Water Everywhere!

Maryland has a close relationship with water. The Atlantic Ocean is a major body of water on the coast of Maryland. In addition, the state is split into two sections by the Chesapeake Bay, which is the United States' largest estuary. An estuary is a partly enclosed body of water where freshwater and seawater mix. The Chesapeake has always been an important feature in Maryland's history and culture. Another major body of water is the Potomac River. This river forms the southwestern and western border of the state. Some other major rivers are the Patapsco, the Patuxent, the Choptank, and the Susquehanna. Although Maryland has many lakes, all of them were created by damming rivers; the state contains no natural lakes.

Maryland's coastline provides a popular place for vacations. Thousands of people enjoy the beach in Ocean City, Maryland, during a typical summer weekend.

Maryland's Natural Regions

Maryland is divided into five main natural regions. One of these regions is the Atlantic Coastal Plain. This area covers about half of the state. Most of the Atlantic Coastal Plain lies east of the Chesapeake Bay in an area called the Eastern Shore. The Eastern Shore lies on a peninsula that also includes parts of Delaware and Virginia. The names of these three states were combined to create a new name: the Delmarva Peninsula. The Eastern Shore is generally flat and marshy, and the land there is very fertile. The Atlantic Coastal Plain

The Wild Ponies of Assateague Island

More than 350 years ago, ponies began roaming Assateague Island, a barrier island on Maryland's Atlantic coast. No one is sure where these wild ponies originated. Some people think they swam to shore after a Spanish ship or a pirate vessel capsized in a storm. Others say they escaped from domesticated herds used in the area for rounding up cattle. Another theory is that the original ponies were brought to the island by colonists who did not want to pay taxes on their livestock. Perhaps all of these stories are true, as different ponies may have joined the herd at different times and for different reasons.

Whatever the explanation, wild ponies soon had the run of the island. Over the years, the herd grew larger and the small, brown-and-white ponies became a common sight. Their thick, shaggy coats helped them survive the strong winds, and they ate island grasses to survive. Although these ponies descended from domestic animals, they have returned to a truly wild state and do not rely on humans to survive.

Today, about three hundred ponies graze on Assateague Island. Half belong to Maryland and half belong to Virginia. A fence divides the herds and the island. The Maryland ponies are managed by the National Park Service. The herd is carefully controlled so that there are not too many ponies for the island to support. The island and its ponies have become a popular tourist attraction, drawing millions. This is a big change from the 1600s, when stray ponies began settling a small, isolated island!

Ponies have roamed Assateague Island for more than 350 years.

also includes land west of the Chesapeake Bay. This area, called the Western Shore, is not as low-lying as the Eastern Shore and contains more forests and gently rolling hills.

The Piedmont Plateau is an upland area of hills and valleys in the middle of the state. This region is filled with rich land that is perfect for dairy farming and raising horses. The boundary between the Piedmont Plateau and the Atlantic Coastal Plain is an area of sharp drops and rough waterfalls known as the fall line. At the fall line, rivers pass from the higher, rockier land of the Piedmont to the lower, sandier land of the coastal plain.

The Blue Ridge region is a narrow region just west of the Piedmont Plateau. It extends from Catoctin Mountain in the east to South Mountain in the west, with a fertile valley in between. The Blue Ridge region marks the eastern edge of the Appalachian Mountains. The Appalachians are a major mountain range that stretches from Alabama to Canada.

Moving farther west in this mountainous area, you'll find the Ridge and Valley region. The valleys of this region contain rich cropland, orchards, marble quarries, and horse farms. This region extends from South Mountain in the east to Dans Mountain in the west.

The Appalachian Plateau covers the westernmost part of the state. This region has forested mountains, cooler temperatures, and beautiful scenery. The Allegheny Mountains, part of the Appalachian mountain range, are located in this region. The Appalachian Plateau contains Maryland's highest point at Backbone Mountain.

Plant Life

Maryland is heavily forested. About 30 percent of the state is covered with forest. More than 150 types of trees are found in the state,

Maryland is working to preserve natural habitats in the Chesapeake Bay. These baby diamondback terrapins hatched from a nest on a restored beach on Poplar Island.

including maple, oak, hemlock, and spruce. The state is also home to a variety of pine trees, including white, Virginia, and loblolly. The wetlands along the Chesapeake Bay have cypress trees as well.

In addition to trees, wild strawberries, raspberries, blackberries, and grapes all grow in the forests of western Maryland. The marshy Eastern Shore features many varieties of grasses, including underwater bay grasses. Wildflowers grow in the forests, fields, and shore areas. The state's flowers include black-eyed Susans, golden asters, honeysuckle, Virginia creeper, swamp pink, and northeastern bulrush.

Animal Life

Maryland is home to a wide range of animals. About 84 species of mammals, 233 species of birds, 85 species of amphibians and reptiles, and 116 species of fish live in Maryland.

Today, the only truly large mammals left in Maryland are a few black bears in the western part of the state. White-tailed deer thrive in the state, and wild horses live on islands near the Atlantic Ocean. Small mammals such as raccoons, squirrels, rabbits, foxes, and skunks live in Maryland's forests and fields.

Many species of birds live in Maryland. Some of these are water birds, such as ducks, geese, swans, great blue herons, sandpipers, plovers, and gulls. There are also many songbirds, such as cardinals, bluebirds, wrens, and doves. Larger birds of prey, such as hawks, peregrine falcons, and bald eagles, also live in Maryland.

Chesapeake Bay hosts a huge variety of marine life. The fish population includes striped bass, alewife, Eastern silvery minnows, and Atlantic needlefish. Crabs, oysters, and clams are also found in the bay, and several different species of turtles live in and around the bay's waters.

Chapter 2

THE HISTORY OF MARYLAND

People have lived in Maryland for at least twelve thousand years. Like most other parts of the United States, Maryland's first residents were Native Americans. The earliest residents are known as the Paleo-Indians. This group arrived at the end of the last ice age, around 10,000 BCE. They lived in movable camps and survived by hunting and fishing. Later groups are known as the Archaic people (7500 BCE–1000 BCE) and the Woodland Indians (1000 BCE–1600 CE). Over thousands of years, these Native Americans became less migratory and established more permanent villages.

Native American Settlers

Another group of Native Americans, called the Algonquians because of the languages they spoke, arrived in Maryland between one thousand and two thousand years ago. These settlers probably migrated from the Great Lakes. They settled in the woods and along the rivers and shores of Maryland. Some important Algonquian tribes in Maryland were the Nanticoke, the Choptank, the Pocomoke, and the Assateague on the Eastern Shore and the Piscataway, the Choptico, and the Yeocomico on the Western Shore. Algonquians were skilled at catching fish and harvesting shellfish. The men hunted and trapped bears, deer, wild turkeys, and other game. The women grew corn, beans, and squash and gathered wild plants, berries, seeds, and nuts.

A different group of Native Americans, called the Susquehannock, lived to the north of the Algonquians. They lived along the Susquehanna River in Maryland, Pennsylvania, and New York. The Susquehannock were enemies of the powerful Iroquois nation located in New York and other areas to the north. During the 1600s, the Iroquois and the Susquehannock were frequently at war. It was a long-term fight that the Iroquois eventually won. Also, the Susquehannock sometimes raided and attacked the Algonquian tribes in the area. They were also involved in vio-

This painting by John White shows Algonquian Indians using nets and spears to catch fish from birch-bark canoes.

lent clashes with colonial settlers on the frontier. A strong nation when the Europeans first arrived, the Susquehannock were eventually killed off by warfare and disease.

The Europeans Arrive

It took some time for Europeans to discover and fully explore the area that is now Maryland. The British became a strong presence in

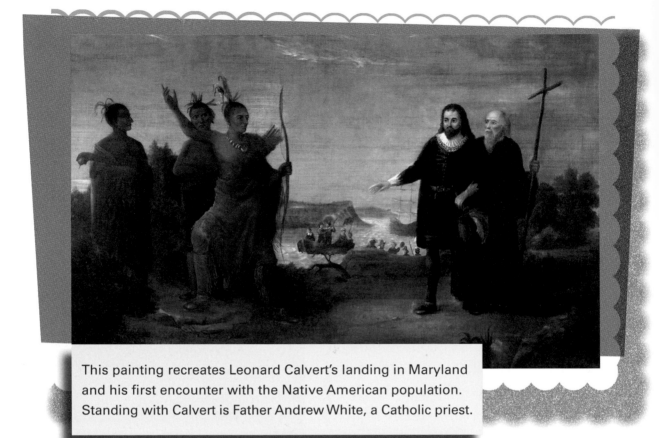

This painting recreates Leonard Calvert's landing in Maryland and his first encounter with the Native American population. Standing with Calvert is Father Andrew White, a Catholic priest.

Maryland in the summer of 1608, when John Smith arrived to explore and map the region. Smith was one of the leaders of Jamestown in nearby Virginia. He sailed all the way up the Chesapeake Bay and explored several thousand miles of its rivers, tributaries, and islands. Smith called the area "the most pleasant place ever known."

In 1631, William Claiborne established the first permanent settlement in Maryland. Claiborne was a British fur trapper and trader, and he built a trading post on Kent Island, near today's city of Annapolis. Claiborne built a profitable business trapping furs and trading with Native Americans.

From Colony to State

In 1632, King Charles I of England granted the land from the Potomac River to the fortieth parallel (near the present site of Philadelphia) to George Calvert, also known as Lord Baltimore. Calvert named the colony "Maryland" after King Charles's wife, Henrietta Maria. However, Calvert died before he could travel to the New World, and the grant was passed on to his son Cecilius. He became the second Lord Baltimore. Cecilius decided to send his younger brother Leonard to lead an expedition of settlers and to be the first governor of the colony. In November 1633, Leonard left England with about 140 settlers and supplies on two ships called the *Ark* and the *Dove*. In March 1634, they landed at St. Clement Island and established the town of St. Mary's. This settlement became the first capital of the colony.

The colony of Maryland was founded with the idea of religious tolerance. The Calverts had become Catholic, and they envisioned the colony as a place where Catholics could practice freely. The freedom to worship was not available in Europe at this time, so many people were attracted to the idea of settling in Maryland, where they could live and worship as they pleased. However, the Catholic settlers were still in the minority in Maryland, and religious conflict flared from time to time.

The colonists established farms, where they grew wheat, corn, beans, and other vegetables and grains. Later, they set up plantations to grow tobacco, which was popular in Europe. Plantations needed a large number of workers, so plantation owners brought indentured servants from England. Later, they brought slaves purchased in the growing African slave trade.

Maryland joined the other twelve colonies in fighting for freedom from Great Britain during the American Revolution. When the war

The Rebirth of Baltimore

In 1904, downtown Baltimore was almost completely destroyed by a huge fire. Afterward, the city was rebuilt, and by World War I it was a thriving, modern city. During the two World Wars, Baltimore relied on steel manufacturing (and other war-related industries) for much of its wealth. The nearby Sparrows Point steel plant and shipyard hummed day and night and provided jobs for immigrants from all over the world. In the 1950s, manufacturing declined. People began moving out of the city, and the population plunged. Even worse, neighborhoods declined as families moved away. By the early 1970s, Baltimore was a shell of its former self, its streets lined with abandoned wrecks of houses.

Today, Baltimore is once again a desirable place to live and to visit. How did this transformation happen? Starting in the 1970s, a group of concerned residents, business owners, and government officials decided to make a change. In 1973, they began a homesteading program, offering abandoned houses to anyone for the price of just $1. People occupied homes again, and neighborhoods began to come alive. Attracted by tax breaks and other incentives, new businesses came to Baltimore, replacing the steel factories that had gone dark.

In addition to rehabilitating neighborhoods, Baltimore reinvented itself as a tourist destination in the 1980s and 1990s. Its waterfront, called the Inner Harbor, was redesigned. Developers built luxury condominiums and opened new hotels. In addition, a new home for the Baltimore Orioles was built at Camden Yards. Today, Baltimore is a revitalized city, and its population continues to grow.

The National Aquarium is the centerpiece of Baltimore's Inner Harbor and a popular tourist attraction.

erupted in 1776, Maryland adopted its own declaration of rights and state constitution. It also sent soldiers and supplies to help in the war. While no Revolutionary battles took place in Maryland, the nickname "Old Line State" refers to its brave line troops who helped in the effort.

On September 17, 1862, the Union Army fought back General Lee's forces at the Battle of Antietam, the bloodiest battle of the Civil War.

On April 28, 1788, Maryland became the seventh state. Soon after, President George Washington, his cabinet, and Congress agreed that the national capital should be centrally located. In 1791, Maryland and Virginia gave land and money to create a territory for the federal capital. Washington chose the specific site along the Potomac River where the capital city (today's Washington, D.C.) would be built.

The Civil War

By the mid-1800s, the northern and southern states were inflamed by the issue of slavery. While northern states banned slavery and felt the practice was immoral, southern states relied on slave labor to run huge plantations and do work in other industries. Although slavery was legal in Maryland, the eastern corridor of the state was an important part of the Underground Railroad. Thousands of slaves made it to the North and to freedom by way of Maryland's Eastern Shore.

In 1861, the issues of slavery and states' rights erupted into the Civil War, which lasted until 1865. Maryland was a border state with conflicting interests. In the end, it did not secede from the Union along with its southern neighbors. However, Maryland's citizens fought on both sides of the conflict. Sadly, many families were torn apart, with brothers, fathers, and sons fighting on opposite sides. Maryland was the site of the Civil War's bloodiest battle, Antietam, which took place on September 17, 1862. More than twenty-three thousand soldiers were killed or wounded. Many smaller battles and skirmishes were also fought in Maryland.

Moving into the Industrial Age

After the war, the state's economy came to rely less on farming and more on industry. Chemical, textile, and canning factories and other businesses grew in urban areas. New railroads were built, such as the Baltimore and Ohio Railroad, the first westward bound passenger railroad in America. The railroads and factories provided jobs to a large number of immigrants who came from Germany, Ireland, Russia, and Poland. In the first half of the twentieth century, the state had shipbuilding and aircraft plants, army bases, and munitions factories important to the government during World War I and World War II.

Today, Maryland continues to be an important industrial center, but it is more involved in service and high-tech areas now. The state is home to a number of biotechnology firms, including pharmaceutical factories. It also boasts important medical and educational institutions, such as Johns Hopkins University. Maryland continues to be an important part of historical events and is a major player in the United States' government and economy.

THE GOVERNMENT OF MARYLAND

Like the federal government, Maryland's state government has three branches. These branches are the executive branch, the legislative branch, and the judicial branch. This system divides powers and responsibilities so that no one leader or part of the government has too much power. The government of Maryland is centered in the state capital, Annapolis.

The Executive Branch

The executive branch carries out the state's laws and runs public affairs. As in other states, the governor is the head of Maryland's executive branch. The governor presides over the Governor's Executive Council, also called the cabinet. The executive council includes twenty department heads who oversee important state agencies. Some of these department heads are the secretary of agriculture, the secretary of business, the secretary of schools, and the secretary of public safety. The governor can also order commissions and task forces to recommend solutions to problems in the state. The governor is elected for a four-year term and can be reelected once.

The lieutenant governor is one of the members of the governor's cabinet. He or she is the governor's second-in-command. Officially,

The Maryland State House in Annapolis is the center of the state's government. Completed in 1779, it is the oldest state house in continuous use for lawmaking and governing.

the lieutenant governor only has the duties that the governor gives him or her. Maryland's lieutenant governor usually attends cabinet meetings, runs various committees, and represents the state at events the governor cannot attend. If the governor leaves office, the lieutenant governor steps in to lead the state.

Other important positions in the executive branch of government include the attorney general, the comptroller, the treasurer, and the secretary of state. The attorney general works closely with the courts to make sure that the state's legal system runs smoothly. The comptroller and the treasurer have control over the state's finances. The secretary of state oversees many different activities and divisions of the executive branch.

The Legislative Branch

The legislative branch in Maryland is called the General Assembly. The General Assembly's job is to make and pass laws. This branch is made up of two houses, the Senate and the House of Delegates.

Maryland's Senate has forty-seven members. Each member represents an area called a legislative district. Senators are elected every four years. The House of Delegates is much larger than the Senate, with 141 members. Each legislative district sends three delegates to the house. Delegates are also elected every four years.

The General Assembly meets for ninety-day sessions. During this time, members must decide the state's budget and create new laws. Senators and delegates serve on one or more committees, such as education or transportation. These committees suggest and review drafts of new laws, which are called bills. A bill must first be approved by its committee. Then it goes before the General Assembly for a vote. Finally, a bill goes to the governor, who can either accept or reject it. If the governor rejects the bill, it can still become a law if three-fifths of the General Assembly votes to pass it again.

The Judicial Branch

The judicial branch is Maryland's court system. It is responsible for trying cases and disputes and for making sure the laws follow the state's constitution. The highest court in the state is the Maryland Court of Appeals (commonly called the supreme court in other states

The Story of Camp David

Camp David is in Catoctin Mountain Park, a rural wilderness area outside of Washington, D.C. In the 1700s and 1800s, European Americans settled the region. They cleared trees to grow crops, build houses, and travel easily. They also used the trees to fuel charcoal furnaces for industry. By the beginning of the twentieth century, many of the mountain slopes were bare.

During the Great Depression in the 1930s, the U.S. government began programs to reclaim the land and regrow the forests. President Franklin D. Roosevelt decided to put people to work building public recreation areas on damaged land. The Catoctin Mountains were selected as one of the sites to be developed. The government purchased the land and hired hundreds of men to build camping and picnicking areas and clear dead trees. New trees began to grow, and the forests returned. Organizations used the camps as places for city dwellers to get away and "return to nature." Camp Misty Mount and Camp Greentop were used for disabled children. Another, Camp Hi-Catoctin, served federal employees and their families.

President Roosevelt often summered at his home in Hyde Park, New York, or spent time on the presidential yacht, *Potomac*. After World War II began, the Secret Service needed to find a safer location for the president to relax. In 1942, Camp Hi-Catoctin was selected and modernized for the president. Roosevelt enjoyed the retreat so much that he called it Shangri-La. In 1952, President Harry S. Truman made the retreat a permanent second home for the president. President Dwight D. Eisenhower renamed it Camp David after his grandson.

Today, Camp David is still a quiet wilderness retreat for the president and First Family, but it has become so much more. It is an important location where the president can contemplate crucial decisions and meet with world leaders on vital issues. Many historic events have occurred at Camp David, including the planning of the Normandy invasion during World War II, meetings between Eisenhower and Soviet leader Nikita Khrushchev, and the negotiation of the Camp David Accords between Israel and Egypt.

and at the federal level). Seven judges serve on the Court of Appeals. These judges are appointed by the governor and confirmed by the Senate for their first term. To serve additional ten-year terms, they must be elected by the state's citizens.

Below the Court of Appeals is the Court of Special Appeals. This court reviews lower court decisions to make sure they are fair. Maryland's lower courts are the district courts and circuit courts. These courts handle local trials, such as those related to murders, robberies, traffic accidents, family matters (like divorce), and civil lawsuits.

The Court of Appeals is Maryland's highest court. Here, seven judges have the final word in deciding if a legal decision is correct.

THE INDUSTRIES OF MARYLAND

Maryland's economy has changed dramatically over the past one hundred years. In the past, most of the state's workforce was employed in manufacturing, agriculture, and fishing. Today, the state's economy is based on service and technology. Maryland has always been prosperous, and it has become even more so in recent decades. In 2007, Maryland had the highest median household income in America.

Service

The service industry is the largest part of Maryland's economy. Many workers make up this industry, including teachers, doctors, salespeople, bankers, computer programmers, and government employees. Because of its location near Washington, D.C., the nation's capital, government employees make up a large part of the service industry. There are a number of military and government-run institutions in Maryland, including Andrews Air Force Base, the U.S. Naval Academy, Fort Meade, the National Institutes of Health, NASA's Goddard Space Flight Center, and the U.S. Weather Bureau. Maryland also has a number of universities, including Johns Hopkins University, an important center of science and medicine.

The U.S. Naval Academy has been located in Maryland since 1845. The graduating class of 2007 watches as the Navy's Blue Angels fly over the ceremony to honor the graduates.

Business and Manufacturing

Business is big in Maryland. The state is home to large corporations such as Marriott International and Perdue. Maryland's manufacturers include the power tool–maker Black & Decker and McCormick & Company, which manufactures spices and syrups for cooking. One of the fastest-growing industries in Maryland is biotechnology. Biotechnology firms create new and useful products in the fields of medicine, agriculture, and the environment, and its workers include research scientists and laboratory workers. Biotechnology has become one of the driving forces in modernizing the state's

Maryland is home to many medical researchers. Above, a scientist at the University of Maryland's Biotechnology Institute does research for a malaria vaccine.

economy. Computers and other consumer electronics are another notable industry, including equipment, software, and support services.

Transportation

With its location on the Chesapeake Bay and the Atlantic Ocean, it is not surprising that Maryland has always been a center of transportation. Baltimore has been an important shipping center since the early 1800s and continues to be one today. The Port of Baltimore is the tenth largest in the United States and can handle everything from cargo ships to cruise ships. The port contributes more than $1 billion a year to the state's economy.

Maryland is also a center of aviation. In 1909, the U.S. Army established its first flight school in College Park. Today, College Park Airport is the world's oldest continuously operating airport. The much larger Baltimore-Washington International Thurgood Marshall Airport (BWI) handles about fifty-five thousand passengers every day. In addition, Lockheed Martin Corporation, a major aerospace company, is headquartered in Bethesda. Lockheed Martin produces military aircraft, missiles, space vehicles, and other products for customers like the U.S. Department of Defense and NASA.

Agriculture

About one-third of the land area of Maryland is used for agriculture. That works out to more than 2 million acres (809,400 hectares). Unlike the huge factory farms in the Midwest, most of Maryland's farms are small. Major products are nursery plants, cut flowers, corn, and soybeans. In addition, Maryland is a major producer of

Past and Present

Good-bye, Tobacco

If you visited Maryland during the 1860s, you would have seen field after field of tobacco plants growing on large plantations. These plantations needed a tremendous number of workers to grow and harvest the crops, so slave labor was used for much of the work. After the Civil War, slavery became illegal in the southern states, and a number of plantations went out of business. Despite the change to paid labor, tobacco was still the main crop in Maryland well into the twentieth century.

However, by the 1960s, people became aware of the dangers of smoking, and the federal government made efforts to decrease smoking. People became even more health-conscious over the years, and by the end of the 1900s, tobacco farming had suffered a serious decline.

Today, tobacco makes up only a small portion of Maryland's agricultural sector. Starting in 2000, the government offered money to any farmer who would grow a crop other than tobacco. Most farmers agreed to this proposal and started growing wine grapes, corn, soybeans, or flowers instead. By 2007, tobacco farming had declined to only 4 percent of what it had been ten years earlier. The crop is not large enough to attract buyers to the tobacco auctions that used to be held in the state, so those auctions no longer take place. Most of the tobacco that is grown in Maryland today is shipped to Europe. The plantation fields growing acres of tobacco are a thing of the past.

Maryland's landscape was once covered with fields of tobacco, like this one in St. Mary's County, photographed in 1942.

chickens, which are used for meat instead of for eggs. Dairy farming is also important, although the number of farms raising cattle is small compared to those raising chickens or crops.

Fishing

It's not surprising that fishing is an important industry in Maryland. Every year, the state produces more than 40 million pounds (18,143,695 kilograms) of seafood. Oysters were once the primary catch, but over the years, disease and damage to oyster beds almost destroyed the oyster population in the Chesapeake Bay. Today, crabs are the biggest part of the state's fishing industry. About half of all

Chesapeake Bay's oyster population has suffered recently, but Maryland residents work hard to cultivate them in the bay.

softshell crabs harvested in the United States come from Maryland. The Maryland blue crab is so important, it was named the state's official crustacean! In addition to employing many people in fishing, the industry provides jobs for people who process, package, and sell the catch.

Chapter 5

PEOPLE FROM MARYLAND:
PAST AND PRESENT

Maryland is the birthplace or home of many great Americans. Here are some of Maryland's most famous and influential citizens.

Benjamin Banneker (1731–1806) Benjamin Banneker was born to freed slaves near Ellicott City. He was a gifted surveyor, astronomer, and mathematician. Banneker's most famous accomplishment was helping survey and plan Washington, D.C.

Eubie Blake (1883–1983) Born in Baltimore in 1883, Eubie Blake started performing as a teenager and went on to become one of the most famous ragtime pianists and composers of the twentieth century. His story was made into a hit Broadway musical, *Eubie!*, in 1978. Blake remained active in music until his death at age one hundred.

Rachel Carson (1907–1964) Although she was born in Pennsylvania, Rachel Carson spent most of her adult life in Silver Spring. A marine biologist and lifelong lover of nature, she worked as a writer for the U.S. Fish and Wildlife Service.

In 1962, she published *Silent Spring*, a book that opened people's eyes to the dangers of pesticides and helped lead the government to ban the insecticide DDT. Carson is a member of the Maryland Women's Hall of Fame.

Rachel Carson dedicated her life to preserving nature and warning people of the dangers of pesticides.

Tom Clancy (1947–) Born in Baltimore in 1947, Tom Clancy is one of today's most popular authors. He specializes in military thrillers. Several of his books, such as *The Hunt for Red October* and *Patriot Games*, have been made into hit movies. Clancy lives in Calvert County.

Frederick Douglass (1817–1895) Frederick Douglass was born into slavery but escaped and became one of the most influential figures of his generation. He edited an abolitionist newspaper, wrote several books, and became a dynamic public speaker and antislavery activist. He also met with President Abraham Lincoln in the White House.

Philip Glass (1937–) Born in Baltimore in 1937, Philip Glass is a noted avant-garde composer. He incorporates

Working Toward Equality

Although many African Americans from Maryland have made notable achievements in the arts, sciences, politics, and other fields, Maryland was not always a place of equal opportunity. Until the late 1950s, the state had segregated schools. Black children and white children had to go to different schools. Black children did not always have well-trained teachers or up-to-date textbooks, and their school buildings were often in poor condition. It was hard for them to get a good education under these conditions.

Discrimination existed all the way up to the college level. In 1935, a student named Donald Murray was prohibited from entering the University of Maryland School of Law because he was black. Murray went to court to win the right to go to the law school, and he won. Murray's case opened the school to other African American students. His lawyer was a Maryland native named Thurgood Marshall, who would go on to even greater accomplishments.

In 1954, Marshall appeared before the Supreme Court to argue against segregation in a case called *Brown v. Board of Education*. The Supreme Court agreed with Marshall that separate schools were unconstitutional. Schools in Maryland, along with schools in other states, began the slow, and often painful, process of integration. Not only did schools begin to integrate, but businesses that had only served whites also began to accept black customers. Like many states, Maryland found it hard in the beginning to integrate its schools and communities. Some whites resisted the changes, and many in the black community became frustrated. A riot in July 1967 left many businesses and a school burned in the small town of Cambridge. The city of Baltimore also struggled to adapt.

Today, all people in Maryland have the same rights and responsibilities. Although opportunities can still be unequal because of poverty and other social problems, segregation is illegal, and all citizens are guaranteed the same rights by law.

Eastern rhythms and elements into his work, creating music that almost puts listeners in a trance. Glass has written symphonies, operas, and film scores. His most famous work is the opera *Einstein on the Beach*.

Matthew Henson (1866–1955) Matthew Henson was born in Charles County in 1866. Orphaned as a child, he worked as a cabin boy on ships and had sailed around the world by the time he was eighteen. In 1909, Henson was one of the first explorers, and the first African American, to reach the North Pole with Admiral Robyn E. Peary.

Billie Holiday (1915–1959) Billie Holiday, who spent her childhood in Baltimore, was one of the greatest jazz and blues singers who ever lived. She poured the pain of her difficult life into her singing. Holiday died in 1959, but her music remained popular, especially after *Lady Sings the Blues*, a hit movie about her life, was released in 1972.

Spike Jonze (1969–) Spike Jonze, whose real name is Adam Spiegel, was born in Rockville and grew up in Bethesda. Jonze started several youth magazines. He has also directed many music and skateboarding videos and commercials, as well as several films. He was nominated for an Academy Award for Best Director for the 1999 film *Being John Malkovich*. Jonze is known for his humorous, quirky, and mind-bending images and ideas.

Thurgood Marshall (1908–1993) Born in Baltimore in 1908, Thurgood Marshall became the first African American

Baltimore native Thurgood Marshall became a towering figure in the civil rights movement and was the first African American to serve on the U.S. Supreme Court.

to serve on the Supreme Court when he was appointed in 1967. Before that, he worked as a lawyer and won twenty-nine cases before the Supreme Court. Many of his cases helped end racial discrimination in education, voting, and housing. His most famous case was the landmark *Brown v. Board of Education* (1954), which led to the desegregation of U.S. public schools.

Phyllis Reynolds Naylor (1933–) Phyllis Naylor has written many popular books for young people. She often tackles difficult subjects, such as mental illness and abuse.

However, she is also known for her popular series about *Alice*, a young girl growing up and facing humorous, everyday problems. In 1992, her novel *Shiloh* won the Newbery Medal for children's literature. Naylor lives in Bethesda and has set several of her books in Maryland.

Cal Ripken Jr. (1960–)
Born in Havre de Grace in 1960, Cal Ripken Jr. is one of the most beloved baseball players of all time. During his career as a shortstop and third baseman for the Baltimore

Cal Ripken Jr. of the Baltimore Orioles set the record for most consecutive games played in professional baseball.

Orioles, Ripken set the record for the most consecutive games—2,632—played in professional baseball. This feat gave Ripken the nickname "Iron Man" and helped gain him induction into the Baseball Hall of Fame in 2007.

Babe Ruth (1895–1948) Born George Herman Ruth in Baltimore, Babe Ruth was raised in an orphanage when his parents were unable to care for him. There he learned to play baseball and went on to an amazing career. While playing for the New York Yankees, he routinely hit more home runs in a season than most other teams. Ruth hit sixty home runs in 1927—a record that was not broken until 1961. His record of

714 career home runs stood until 1974. Ruth was one of the original inductees into the Baseball Hall of Fame in 1936.

Robert Sargent Shriver Jr. (1915–) Sargent Shriver was born in Westminster. He was the brother-in-law of President John F. Kennedy and is the father of Maria Shriver. Shriver served under Kennedy as the first director of the Peace Corps, a service organization that helps people around the world. He is also responsible for creating socially conscious programs such as VISTA, Head Start, Foster Grandparents, Job Corps, and more.

Upton Sinclair (1878–1968) The novelist and social critic Upton Sinclair was born in Baltimore in 1878. His most famous work, *The Jungle* (published in 1906), portrayed the brutal and unsanitary conditions of the meatpacking industry. Sinclair's book was so shocking that it led Congress to pass the Pure Food and Drug Act and the Meat Inspection Act.

Jada Pinkett Smith (1971–) Born in Baltimore in 1971, Jada Pinkett Smith has appeared in popular films such as *The Nutty Professor*, and she provided a voice in the animated *Madagascar* movies. She is married to superstar actor Will Smith and is the mother of a new generation of actors: daughter Willow and son Jaden.

Harriet Tubman (1820-1913) Harriet Tubman was born on the Eastern Shore in 1820. After enduring a difficult life as a slave, she escaped—and then went back to rescue others.

Tubman became a leading figure on the Underground Railroad and led more than three hundred slaves to freedom. Later, she worked as a nurse, spy, and scout for the Union Army during the Civil War and became a noted public speaker in the North. Tubman moved to New York, where she died in 1913.

Frank Zappa (1940–1993) Frank Zappa was born in Baltimore in 1940. He was an influential rock guitarist, singer, and song-writer and is most famous for his eccentric musical styles and satirical lyrics. Zappa died in 1993.

After escaping a brutal life as a slave, Harriet Tubman led more than three hundred other slaves to freedom in the North.

Timeline

10,000 BCE	The first Native Americans arrive in Maryland.
1608	Captain John Smith explores the Chesapeake Bay and the Potomac River.
1631	William Claiborne establishes a trading post on Kent Island. It is the first permanent European settlement in Maryland.
1632	King Charles I of England grants George Calvert, Lord Baltimore, a charter for the colony of Maryland.
1634	Leonard Calvert leads 140 settlers to Maryland and establishes St. Mary's City.
1649	Maryland passes the Religious Toleration Act.
1664	Maryland passes a law allowing slavery.
1694	Maryland's capital is moved from St. Mary's City to Annapolis.
1729	The city of Baltimore is founded as Baltimore Town.
1767	The Mason-Dixon Line is established to settle a border dispute with Pennsylvania.
1776	Maryland establishes a state government at the start of the American Revolution.
1781	Maryland becomes the thirteenth and final state to ratify the Articles of Confederation.
1784	Congress ratifies the Treaty of Paris, ending the Revolutionary War, in Annapolis.
1788	Maryland becomes the seventh state to ratify the Constitution.
1791	Maryland donates land for the federal capital of the United States. This area later becomes known as the District of Columbia.
1814	During the War of 1812, Francis Scott Key writes "The Star-Spangled Banner," which later becomes the national anthem.
1838	Frederick Douglass escapes from slavery in Baltimore.
1845	The U.S. Naval Academy is founded at Annapolis.
1861	The Civil War begins, with Maryland staying in the Union.

1862	The Battle of Antietam, the bloodiest of the Civil War, is fought near Sharpsburg.
1864	Maryland abolishes slavery.
1865	The Civil War ends with a Union victory.
1873	Philanthropist Johns Hopkins leaves $8 million to start both a university and a hospital.
1886	The Enoch Pratt Free Library, gift of philanthropist Enoch Pratt, opens in Baltimore.
1904	A fire destroys seventy blocks in Baltimore's business district.
1935	University of Maryland School of Law is opened to African Americans after lawyer Thurgood Marshall wins the case of Donald Murray.
1967	Thurgood Marshall becomes the first African American Supreme Court justice.
1973	Baltimore begins efforts to clean up slums by selling abandoned houses for $1 apiece.
1981	The National Aquarium opens in Baltimore.
1983	Maryland and other states sign the Chesapeake Bay Agreement to restore the health of the bay.
2000	Chesapeake 2000, the renewed bay agreement, is signed.
2006	Maryland lawmakers pass the Healthy Air Act to reduce the emissions of pollutants from the state's power plants.
2007	A Middle East peace conference is held at the U.S. Naval Academy in Annapolis.
2009	Racehorse Rachel Alexandra becomes the first filly since 1924 to win the Preakness Stakes, held at Pimlico Race Course.

Maryland at a Glance

State motto	"Manly Deeds, Womanly Words"
State capital	Annapolis
State flower	Black-eyed Susan
State bird	Baltimore oriole
State tree	White oak
State crustacean	Maryland blue crab
Statehood date and number	April 28, 1788; the seventh state
State nicknames	Old Line State; Free State
Total area and U.S. rank	12,193 sq mi (31,580 sq km); forty-second largest state
Population	5,296,516 (2000 census)
Length of coastline	31 miles (50 km) on the Atlantic Ocean
Highest elevation	Hoye Crest at Backbone Mountain, 3,360 feet (1024 m)
Lowest elevation	Sea level, at the Atlantic Ocean

State Flag

State Seal

Major rivers	Potomac River, Susquehanna River, Patuxent River, Chester River, Nanticoke River, Patapsco River
Major lakes	Deep Creek Lake, Liberty Lake, Prettyboy Lake
Hottest temperature recorded	109 degrees Fahrenheit (43 degrees Celsius), at Allegheny County on July 3, 1898, and at Cumberland and Frederick on July 10, 1936
Coldest temperature recorded	-40°F (-40°C), at Oakland on January 13, 1912
Origin of state name	Queen Henrietta Maria, wife of King Charles I of England
Chief agricultural products	Nursery plants and flowers, corn, tobacco, milk, poultry, hogs, dairy cattle
Major industries	Service, technology, shipping, agriculture, fishing

Baltimore oriole

Black-eyed Susan

GLOSSARY

agriculture The practice of farming.

biotechnology Creating new products in the fields of medicine, agriculture, etc., by using and changing living organisms.

circuit court Court that operates on the local level.

constitution Basic laws that establish and run a government and that guarantee certain rights to the people.

desegregation Removing any law or practice that requires people to be separated because of their race.

domesticated Adapted to live in close association with, and to be used by, humans.

economy A system for the production and buying and selling of goods and services.

estuary A partly enclosed coastal body of water where freshwater and saltwater mix.

executive The branch of a state or federal government that runs public affairs and carries out the laws.

federal Having to do with the national government.

homesteading A system that encourages people to live in an area by offering homes or land to them for free or at a greatly reduced price.

immigrant Person who leaves one country to live in another country.

indentured servant Person who agrees to work for a master for a specified time in return for payment of travel expenses.

integration Incorporating people of different races or groups as equals into an organization or society.

judicial Having to do with judges and courts.

legislative Having to do with making laws.

migratory Roving; nomadic; wandering.

peninsula A portion of land surrounded by water on three sides.

pharmaceutical Having to do with drugs that are used for medical reasons.

plantation A large farm located in the southern United States that usually grew tobacco or cotton.

ratify To approve or confirm formally.

satirical Given to exposing or criticizing through humor or irony.

secede To withdraw from an organization.

territory A geographic area belonging to a government.

textile Cloth.

tolerance Allowing people to think and behave as they want.

Baltimore Museum of Industry

1415 Key Highway

Inner Harbor South

Baltimore, MD 21230

(410) 727-4808

Web site: http://www.thebmi.org

This museum preserves Maryland's industrial, maritime, and labor heritage. Exhibits and archives show what it was like to work in industries such as oyster canning, printing, garment making, and more.

Fort McHenry National Monument and Historic Shrine

2400 East Fort Avenue

Baltimore, MD 21230-5393

(410) 962-4290

Web site: http://www.nps.gov/fomc

This national park has restored barracks and military memorabilia that show the fort's role in American history. The new Fort McHenry Library has additional historical information.

Greater Baltimore Committee

111 South Calvert Street, Suite 1700

Baltimore, MD 21202

(410) 727-2820

Web site: http://www.gbc.org

This organization of civil and business leaders is dedicated to improving opportunities and daily life in Baltimore, Maryland's largest city.

Maryland Historical Society

201 West Monument Street

Baltimore, MD 21201

(410) 685-3750

Web site: http://www.mdhs.org

The historical society has information, photographs, and additional archival material about Maryland's history.

Maryland Office of Tourism Development

401 East Pratt Street, 14th Floor

Baltimore, MD 21202

(866) 639-3526

Web site: http://www.visitmaryland.org

You can learn about the many interesting things to see and do in Maryland through this organization.

Office of the Governor

Maryland State House

100 State Circle

Annapolis, MD 21401

(410) 974-3901

Web site: http://www.gov.state.md.us

The official Web site of the state governor includes information on current events, goals, and policies.

Web Sites

Due to the changing nature of Internet links, Rosen Publishing has developed an online list of Web sites related to the subject of this book. This site is updated regularly. Please use this link to access this list:

http://www.rosenlinks.com/uspp/mdpp

Doak, Robin. *Voices from Colonial America: Maryland 1634–1776*. Washington, DC: National Geographic, 2007.

Heinrichs, Ann, and Matt Kania. *Maryland*. Mankato, MN: Child's World, 2005.

Marsh, Carole. *Maryland Native Americans: A Kid's Look at Our State's Chiefs, Tribes, Reservations, Powwows, Lore and More from the Past to the Present*. Peachtree City, GA: Gallopade International, 2004.

Menendez, Shirley. *B is for Blue Crab: A Maryland Alphabet*. Chelsea, MI: Sleeping Bear Press, 2004.

Mills, Claudia. *The Totally Made-Up Civil War Diary of Amanda MacLeish*. New York, NY: Farrar, Straus and Giroux, 2008.

Mis, Melody A. *The Colony of Maryland: A Primary Source History*. New York, NY: PowerKids Press, 2006.

Naylor, Phyllis Reynolds. *All but Alice*. New York, NY: Aladdin MIX, 2008.

Naylor, Phyllis Reynolds. *Cricket Man*. New York, NY: Atheneum, 2008.

Naylor, Phyllis Reynolds. *Starting with Alice*. New York, NY: Atheneum, 2002.

Paterson, Katherine. *The Great Gilly Hopkins*. New York, NY: Crowell, 1978.

Paterson, Katherine. *Jacob Have I Loved*. New York, NY: Crowell, 1980.

Somervill, Barbara A. *Maryland*. New York, NY: Children's Press, 2003.

Sonneborn, Liz. *A Primary Source History of the Colony of Maryland*. New York, NY: Rosen Publishing Group, Inc., 2006.

Sterngass, Jon. *Frederick Douglass*. New York, NY: Chelsea House Publishers, 2009.

Tayac, Gabrielle. *Meet Naiche: A Native Boy from the Chesapeake Bay Area*. Milwaukee, WI: Gareth Stevens Publishing, 2004.

Walker, Sally M. *Life in an Estuary*. Minneapolis, MN: Lerner Publications Co., 2003.

Walker, Sally M. *Written in Bone: Buried Lives of Jamestown and Colonial Maryland*. Minneapolis, MN: Carolrhoda Books, 2009.

Wimmer, Teresa. *Maryland*. Mankato, MN: Creative Education, 2009.

BIBLIOGRAPHY

Assateague Naturalist. "The Ponies on Assateague." Assateague.com. Retrieved April 15, 2009 (http://assateague.com/pony.html).

Blashfield, Jean F. *Maryland*. New York, NY: Scholastic, 2008.

Chartock, Lea Susan. "Oyster Industry in the Chesapeake Bay." Maryland Online Encyclopedia. Retrieved May 25, 2009 (http://www.mdoe.org/oyster_indus.html).

Chesapeake Bay Program. "About the Bay." ChesapeakeBay.net. Retrieved April 15, 2009 (http://www.chesapeakebay.net/aboutbay.aspx?menuitem=13953).

Clark, Wayne E. "The Algonquian Speaking Indians of Maryland." Maryland Online Encyclopedia. Retrieved June 15, 2009 (http://www.mdoe.org/algonquian.html).

Fergus, Charles, and Amelia Hansen. *Wildlife of Virginia and Maryland and Washington, D.C.* Mechanicsburg, PA: Stackpole Books, 2003.

History Empire. "Camp David." American-Presidents.com. Retrieved April 20, 2009 (http://www.american-presidents.com/camp-david).

Koenig, Karl W. "Blake, James Hubert 'Eubie' (1883-1983)." Maryland Online Encyclopedia. Retrieved June 20, 2009 (http://www.mdoe.org/blakeeubie.html).

Kotlowski, Dean. "Carson, Rachel (1907–1964)." Maryland Online Encyclopedia. Retrieved June 17, 2009 (http://www.mdoe.org/carsonrachel.html).

Maryland State Archives. "Maryland at a Glance: Government." April 15, 2009. Retrieved July 14, 2009 (http://www.msa.md.gov/msa/mdmanual/01glance/html/govern.html).

Maryland State Archives. "Maryland at a Glance: State Symbols." October 1, 2008. Retrieved July 12, 2009 (http://www.msa.md.gov/msa/mdmanual/01glance/html/symbols/00list.html).

McCarthy, Michael P. "Baltimore Urban Renewal." Maryland Online Encyclopedia. Retrieved June 15, 2009 (http://www.mdoe.org/urbanrenewinnerharb.html).

Rucker, Philip. "End of an Era for Maryland Tobacco." *Washington Post*, March 1, 2007.

Shivers, Frank R., Jr. "Introduction to Baltimore." Baltimore City Historical Society, 2003. Retrieved June 16, 2009 (http://www.historicbaltimore.org/resources/shivers/intro.htm).

U.S. National Park Service. "Catoctin Mountain Park: Presidential Retreat." Retrieved July 22, 2009 (http://www.nps.gov/cato/historyculture/retreat.htm).

Williams, Juan. "Marshall, Thurgood (1908–1993)." Maryland Online Encyclopedia. Retrieved June 21, 2009 (http://www.mdoe.org/marshall_thur.html).

About the Author

Joanne Mattern is captivated by Maryland's rich history and culture—not to mention its delicious food! She enjoys history, nature, travel, and discovering new places and interesting stories. She has written more than two hundred nonfiction books for children and also works in her local library. Mattern lives in New York State with her husband, four children, and a menagerie of pets.

Photo Credits

Cover (top, left), pp. 17, 28, 37 Library of Congress Prints & Photographs Division; cover (top, right) Mark Wilson/Getty Images; cover (bottom) Vic Bider/Stone/Getty Images; pp. 3, 6, 12, 19, 20, 24, 30, 38–39, 41 Wikipedia; p. 4 © GeoAtlas; pp. 7, 10, 23, 26, 29 © AP Images; p. 8 © www.istockphoto.com/Jennifer Dodge; p. 13 Erich Lessing/Art Resource, NY; p. 14 Courtesy of the Maryland Historical Society; p. 16 © James Lemass/SuperStock; p. 25 Shannon O'Connor/U.S. Navy; p. 31 Alfred Eisenstaedt/Time & Life Pictures/Getty Images; p. 34 Hank Walker/Time & Life Pictures/Getty Images; p. 35 Ronald C. Modra/Sports Imagery/Getty Images; p. 40 (left) Courtesy of Robesus, Inc.

Designer: Les Kanturek; Editor: Andrea Sclarow;
Photo Researcher: Amy Feinberg